Northamptonshire County Council
Libraries and

NOV

04. JUN 97

DISCARDED Libraries

PAID

ROBSON, D.   19. JUL

Masks and funny faces

This book is due for return on or before the last date shown above but it may be renewed by personal application, post, or telephone, quoting this date and details of the book.

Northamptonshire Libraries and Information Service

00 300 617 208

RAINY DAYS
MASKS
AND
FUNNY FACES

DENNY ROBSON

FRANKLIN WATTS
LONDON · NEW YORK · TORONTO · SYDNEY

CONTENTS

Party masks	4
Paper plate masks	8
Robot	12
Bright-eyed robot	14
Paper bag masks	16
Papier mâché masks	20
Bits and pieces	24
Face painting	28
All together!	30
Tracing and index	32

Northamptonshire Libraries

J

Design: David West
  Children's Book Design
Designer: Flick Killerby
Photography: Roger Vlitos
Editor: Denny Robson

© Aladdin Books Ltd 1991

Created and designed by
N.W. Books Ltd
28 Percy Street
London W1P 9FF

First published in
Great Britain in 1991 by
Franklin Watts Ltd
96 Leonard Street
London EC2A 4RH

ISBN 0 7496 0615 0

A CIP catalogue record for this book is available from the British Library

All rights reserved

Printed in Belgium

Introduction

Masks have been used for hundreds of years, for lots of different reasons. Warriors have worn masks in battle to make them look fierce. Medicine men and witch doctors used masks in ceremonies to make them look more mysterious. And in some countries, actors still wear masks to help the audience distinguish different characters.

But wearing a mask doesn't just make you look different. It can make you feel different too. Behind a mask you can become more confident, or turn into another character altogether!

Some of the masks in this book are very simple and can be made quite quickly. Others will take more time and you may need the help of an older person. But all are great fun, both to make and wear.

These are some of the materials used to make the masks in this book. You will probably be able to find most things in your home. Before you begin, check the materials needed and gather everything together. It's also a good idea to cover your work surface with newspaper before you start.

Party masks

These half masks are very simple to make. You could make several to give to friends at a party. Or you could get your guests to design and make their own mask as one of the party games. All of the masks on the next few pages can be traced. If you need help with tracing, turn to page 32.

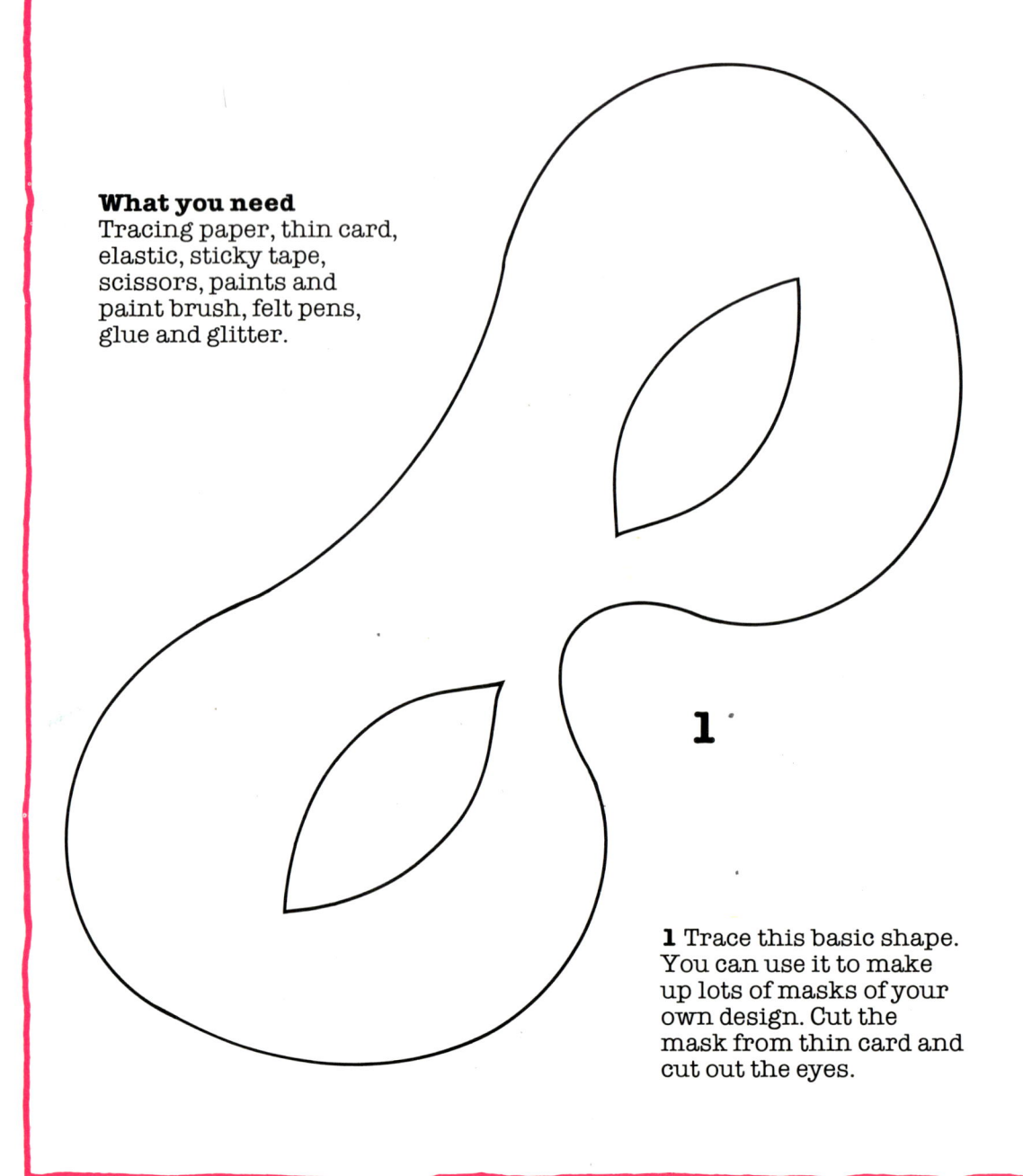

What you need
Tracing paper, thin card, elastic, sticky tape, scissors, paints and paint brush, felt pens, glue and glitter.

1 Trace this basic shape. You can use it to make up lots of masks of your own design. Cut the mask from thin card and cut out the eyes.

2 This harlequin mask has been brightly painted. It would also look effective decorated with pieces of gummed coloured paper.

3 Measure a piece of elastic to go around the back of your head. When the paint is quite dry, attach the elastic to the back of the mask with sticky tape.

Party masks

Here are four other designs for you to try. Make sure you use good thick paint for a really bold result.

Madame Butterfly
Use this shape for your outline and then decorate the butterfly as you wish. Felt pens are good for more detailed designs.

Goggles
These strange goggles make an unusual mask for budding pilots.

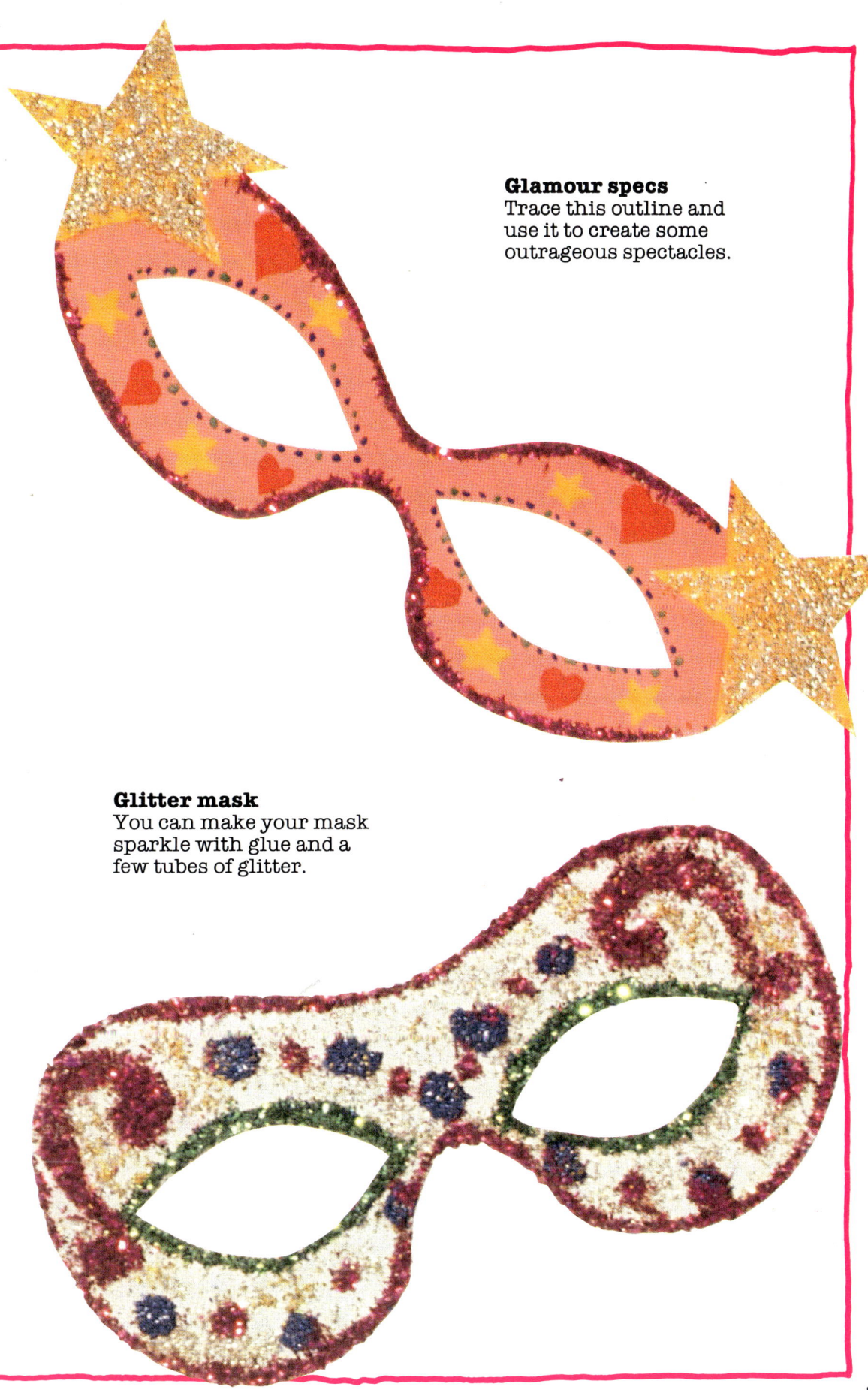

Glamour specs
Trace this outline and use it to create some outrageous spectacles.

Glitter mask
You can make your mask sparkle with glue and a few tubes of glitter.

Paper plate masks

Paper plates are a quick and easy way of making masks that cover your whole face. They can either be tied to your head with elastic, as with the party masks, or you can glue a stick to the back and hold them in front of your face. Experiment with different designs. You can decorate them with scrap materials, such as wool, dried pasta shapes, sequins and beads, as well as with paint.

What you need
Paper plates, elastic or sticks, sticky tape, glue, paints, tissue paper, string, an egg box and scissors.

1 Look in a mirror and carefully measure the distance between your eyes. Mark these points about half way down the paper plate.

2 Make the eye holes by pushing a pencil through the marked points.

3 Attach elastic to fit your head, as before.

3

4 Paint the face. It could be happy, sad, funny or fierce, depending on how you feel.

4

Paper plate masks

Sunflower
This pretty mask looks very effective, but it's not difficult to make. First paint the plate a cheery yellow. Make the eye holes and outline with green. Cut 'petals' from yellow and orange tissue paper and then glue them to each side of the plate so that they overlap. Finally, give the flower a smile.

Cyclops

You can make all sorts of monsters out of paper plates. To make this scary Cyclops, first paint a paper plate blue. Then scrunch up pieces of blue tissue paper and glue them to the plate. Cyclops' eye and mouth are cut from an egg box and painted. His eyelashes are pink tissue paper. Lastly, add blue string to make his untidy hair.

Robot

Three-dimensional masks that fit over your head can be very exciting. This robot is made from a very large cardboard box. It has armholes so that it fits over your head and shoulders, but a box which covers just your head would also work well. To make this robot even more spectacular, find out how to give him eyes which light up on page 14.

What you need
Cardboard box, paper plates, toilet roll, small oblong box, silver foil, sticky tape and a piece of wire.

1 If the box is very large, cut armholes in the sides as shown.

2 Cover with silver foil, securing it with sticky tape at the edges.

3 Cut the eyes and nose from a toilet roll. Use a small box for the mouth. Cover with silver foil. Make the ears from a paper plate, as shown. Tape all features to the box.

4 For the antenna, cover a paper plate with foil. Push one end of the wire through the plate and wind the rest of the wire round a strip of foil. Push through the top of the box.

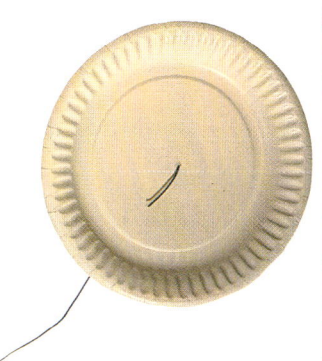

Bright-eyed robot

What you need
One long piece of electrical wire (A), 2 pieces half this length (B,C), 1 short piece (D), 2 paper clips, 2 small bulbs, 2 small batteries and sticky tape.

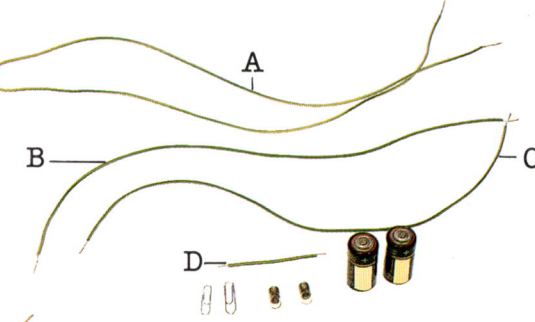

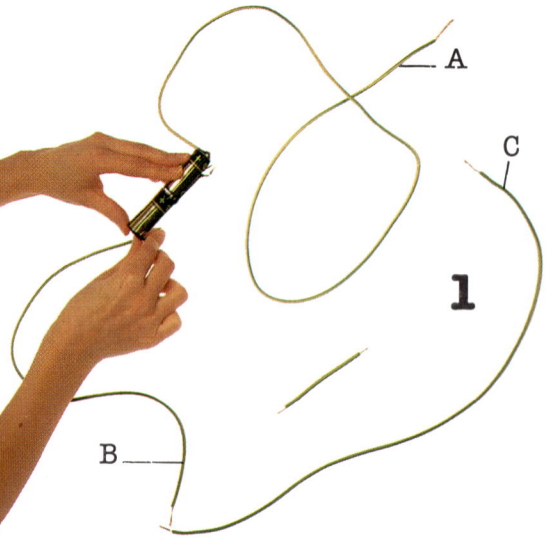

1 Tape the two batteries together, positive to negative. Tape wire A to one end of the batteries and wire B to the other.

2 Tape the batteries inside the box at the bottom. Make a small hole above each of the robot's eyes. Push wire A through one of the holes to the front.

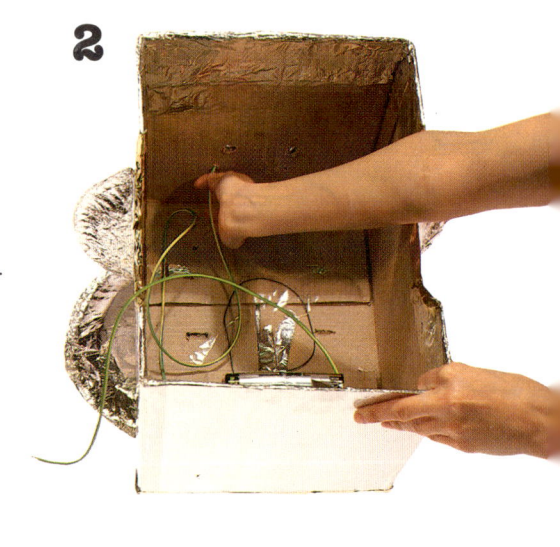

3 Push wire C through the other hole to the front of the box. Wire B will be used later to make the switch.

14

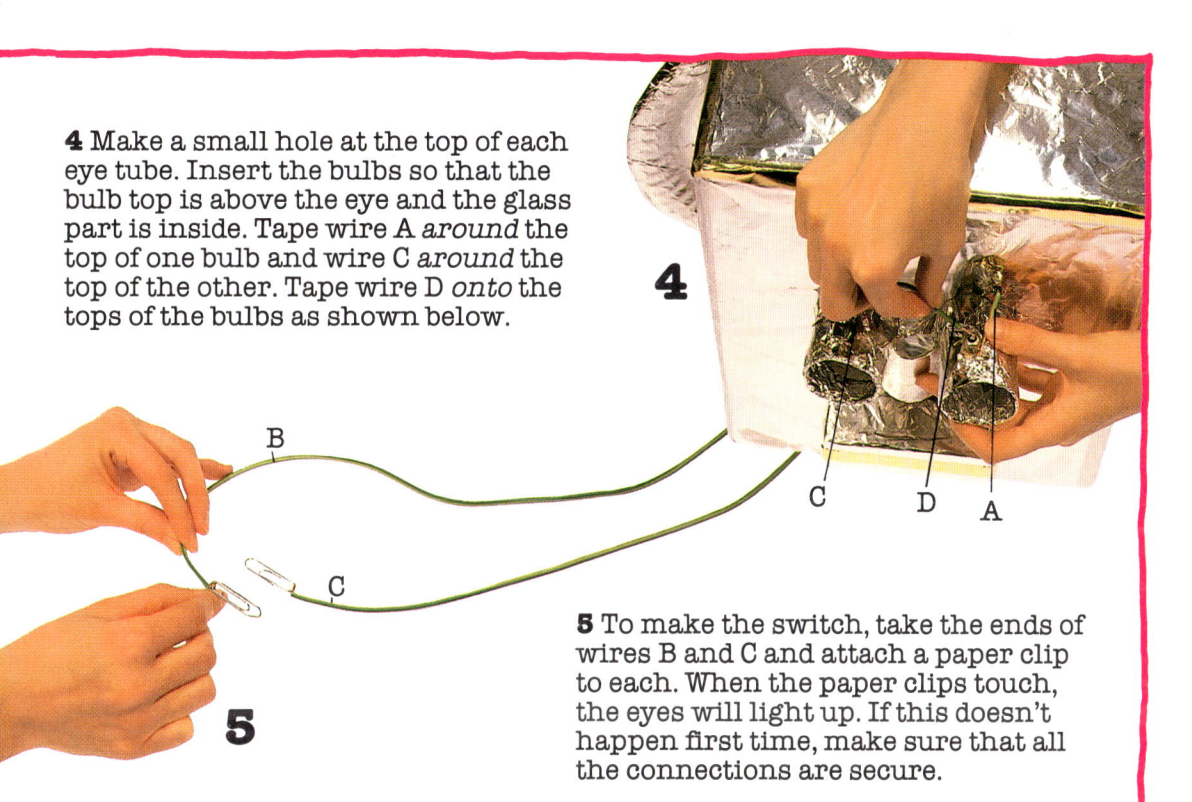

4 Make a small hole at the top of each eye tube. Insert the bulbs so that the bulb top is above the eye and the glass part is inside. Tape wire A *around* the top of one bulb and wire C *around* the top of the other. Tape wire D *onto* the tops of the bulbs as shown below.

5 To make the switch, take the ends of wires B and C and attach a paper clip to each. When the paper clips touch, the eyes will light up. If this doesn't happen first time, make sure that all the connections are secure.

15

Paper bag masks

Paper bags are an excellent way to make really effective masks and head-dresses. It doesn't matter if the bag is plain or printed. Poster paints should cover over any pattern. Just make sure that the bag fits your head before you start.

WARNING: Do not use plastic bags as they are extremely dangerous.

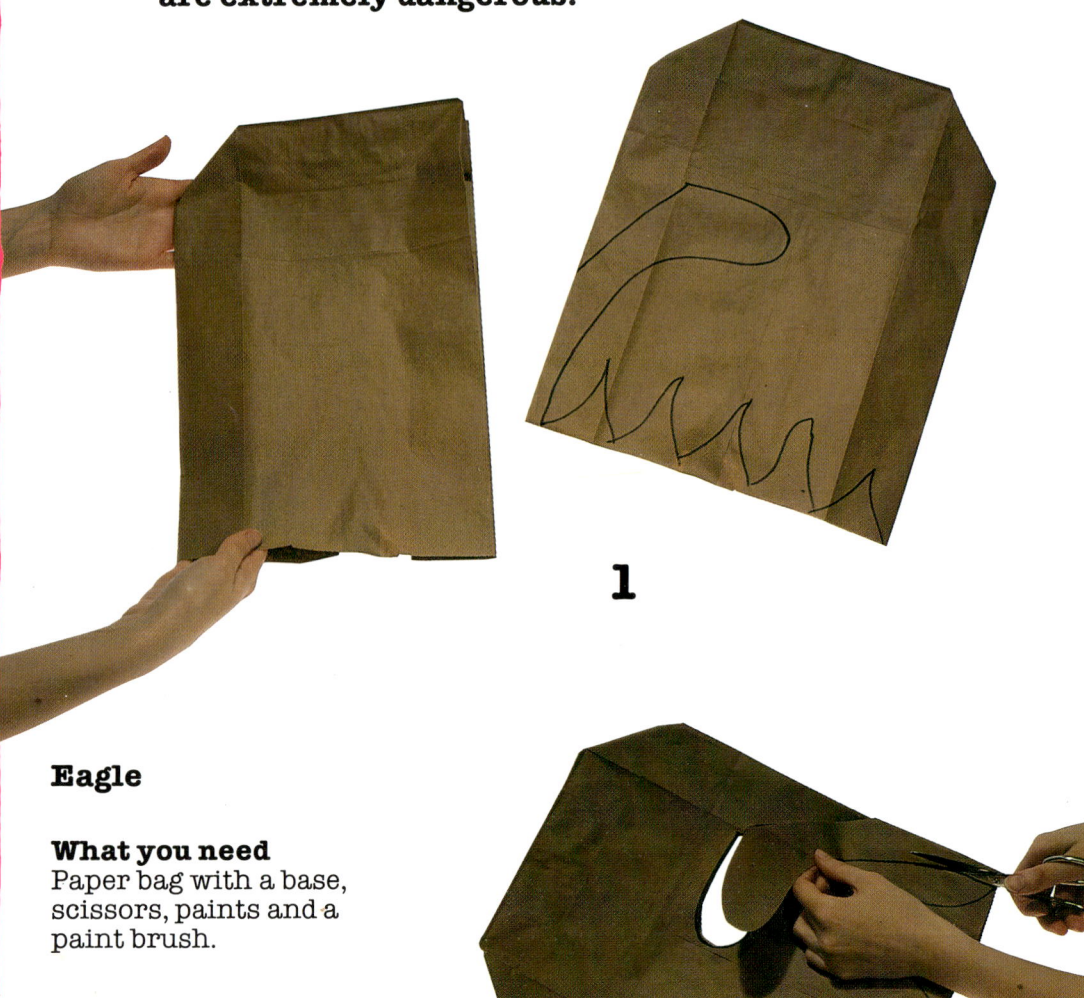

1

Eagle

What you need
Paper bag with a base, scissors, paints and a paint brush.

1 Flatten the bag with the base tucked inside. Draw the outline.

2 Cut between the beak and feathers, as shown.

2

3 Outline the features in black and then colour in with bright paints.

4 Wait until the paint is dry and then cut out the feathers at the base. Wear the head-dress with the feathers open, or clip them together under your chin.

Paper bag masks

The Rooster
The rooster mask is made in the same way as the eagle. Again, the base of the bag provides the beak.

What you need
Paper bag with a base, orange card, glue, scissors, paints and a paint brush.

1 Draw the outline and cut out between the beak and feathers. Cut shapes from orange card, as shown.

2 Glue the rooster's comb to the inside of the folded base and glue the other shapes to the sides. Finally, paint the rooster, outlining the eyes and beak.

The Frog
The frog mask has prominent eyes and a long curly tongue for catching flies!

What you need
Paper bag with a base, pink tissue paper, a piece of wire, scissors, paints and a paint brush.

1 Cut out the mouth and around the neck. Make cuts as indicated in the base of the bag. Fold in the base either side of these cuts to make the eyes.

2 Cover the wire with the strips of tissue to make the tongue. Bend and stick in place. Paint the frog, outlining the eyes.

Papier mâché masks

Papier mâché is French for mashed paper. It is made by soaking paper in paste and then drying it in a particular shape. It's fun to make, but quite messy so be sure to cover your work surface (and your clothes!) before you start. Here we show you how to make a mask shell which can be made into a mouse or an elephant.

What you need
Flour, water, mixing bowl, spoon, strips of newspaper, balloon and a plastic bowl.

1

1 Mix enough flour with water to make a thick, creamy paste.

2

2 Stand a large balloon in a plastic bowl to keep it steady. Soak the newspaper strips in paste and cover the balloon with them.

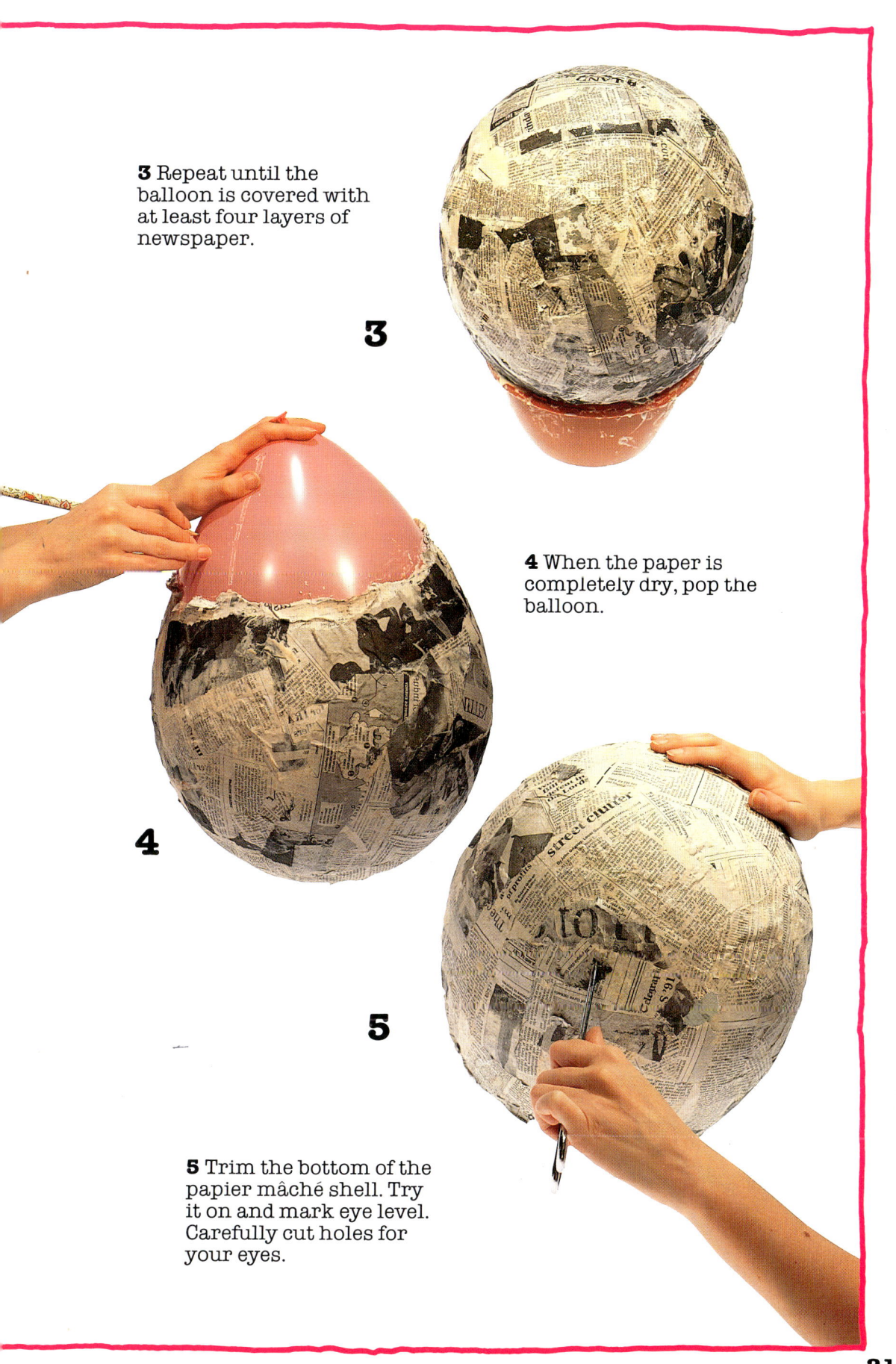

3 Repeat until the balloon is covered with at least four layers of newspaper.

3

4 When the paper is completely dry, pop the balloon.

4

5

5 Trim the bottom of the papier mâché shell. Try it on and mark eye level. Carefully cut holes for your eyes.

Papier mâché

What you need
Brown card, pink paper, 2 strips of card, white paper, egg box, scissors, glue, paints and a paint brush.

The mouse
Paint the papier mâché shell, as shown. Stick on squares of white paper for the teeth. The nose is a section cut from an egg box.

Make the whiskers by twisting rolls of white paper.

To make the ears curved, make a small cut at the base of each ear. Overlap and glue. Cover each ear with the pink paper shapes. Glue the features to the mouse.

22

What you need
Wool, grey tissue paper, 2 strips of card, 4 yoghurt cartons, (washing-up liquid will help paint stick to the cartons), string, glue, sticky tape, scissors, paints and a paint brush.

The elephant
Paint the shell and when it is quite dry, glue on wool hair and eyelashes. Make ears from tissue paper, strengthened at the top by a strip of card. Make the trunk by threading 4 painted yoghurt cartons on a piece of string, as shown. Add the ears and trunk to the shell.

Bits and pieces

You don't have to wear a complete mask to change your identity. It can be fun just to make various 'props' for your face. You could mix them up to create weird and wonderful disguises. The bits and pieces on this page are all worn attached to a circle of card which fits your head. Turn the page to see them in action!

For each 'prop' you will need a card head band. Cut a piece of string the size of your head. Make the circle of card using this as a measure.

Mouse ears
Make the ears as shown on page 22 and stick them to the band with double-sided tape.

King Tut
King Tut is made from just one piece of card and then cleverly painted. Don't forget holes for the eyes.

Clown
The clown's hat and glasses are attached to two separate head bands.

Pirate
This pirate hat and eye patch make a quick and easy fancy dress costume.

25

Bits and pieces

Mouse

King Tut

26

Pirate

Clown

27

Face painting

You can create a very special mask with face paints. It comes alive as you change your expressions! Try the designs we have suggested on the next few pages and then experiment with some of your own. Whether you attempt a tiger, butterfly, clown or monster, keep the design simple for the most dramatic result.

What you need
Face paints (which can be bought quite cheaply at most toy shops), paint brush, sponge, cleansing cream or soap and water to remove.

Skeleton
1 Prepare yourself or your model before you start. Apply white paint all over the face, using the sponge or your fingers to blend.

1

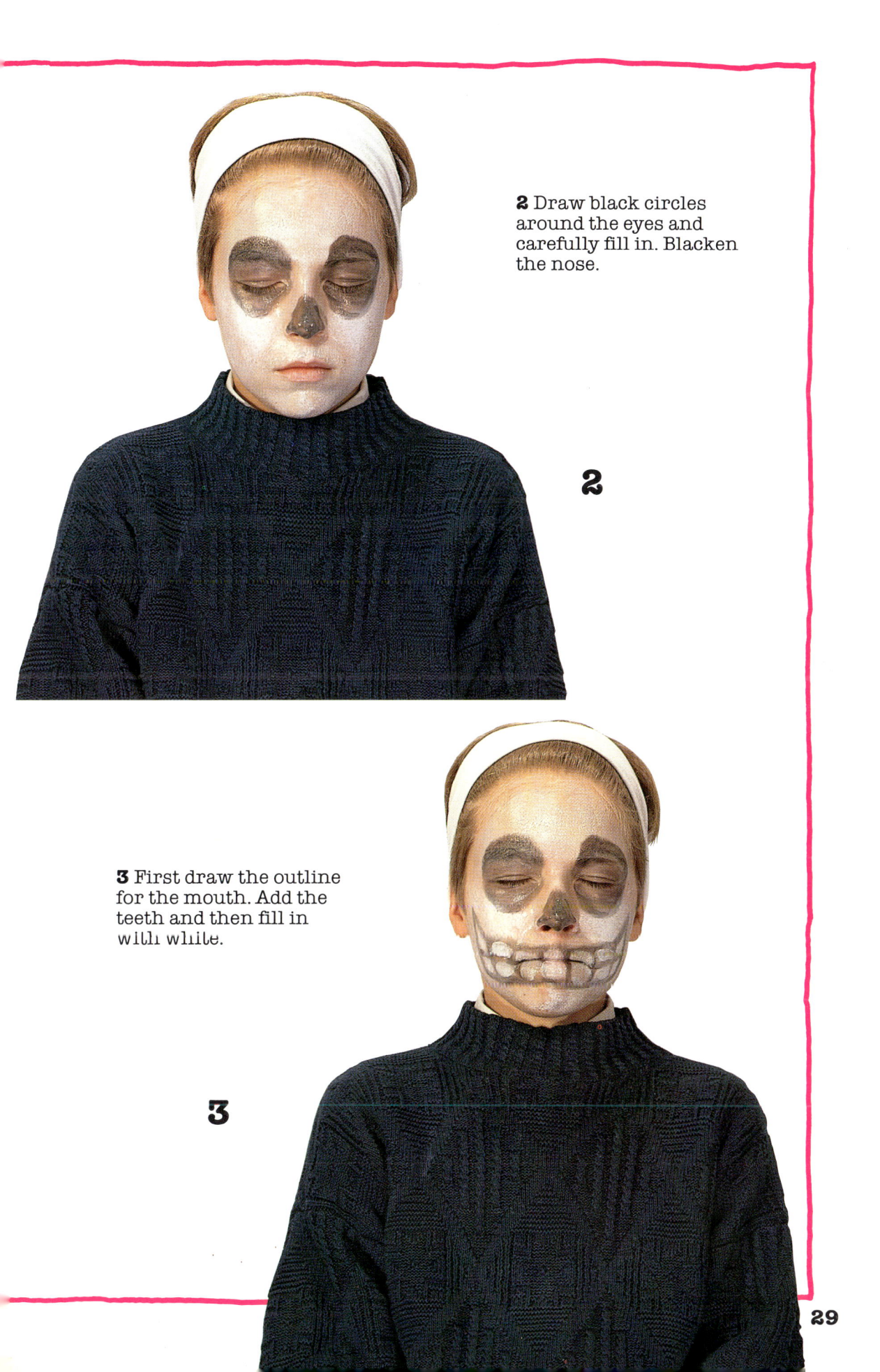

2 Draw black circles around the eyes and carefully fill in. Blacken the nose.

2

3 First draw the outline for the mouth. Add the teeth and then fill in with white.

3

All together!

If you combine masks or face props with a little face painting, your disguise becomes even more effective. You don't need a lot of detail. A few whiskers here or a little war paint there can make all the difference. You may need to warm the face crayons in your hand before you start, or you may find it easier to apply them with a paint brush.

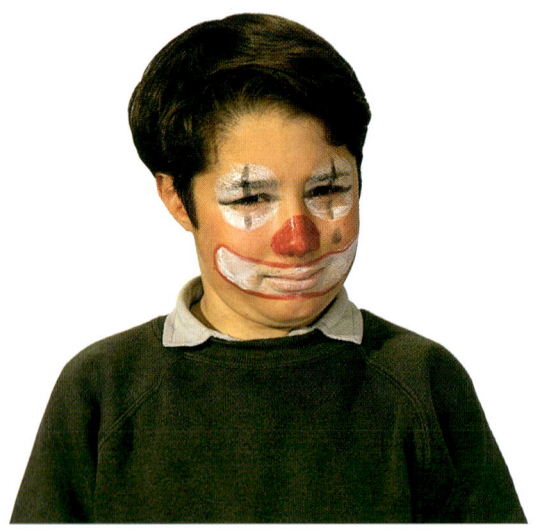

Mouse
Put on the ears and add two long teeth, a nose, cheeks and whiskers to complete the look.

Clown
Cross the eyes and then make your clown happy or sad with a wide painted mouth.

Eagle
The eagle turns into a red indian's head-dress when you add a few stripes of war paint.

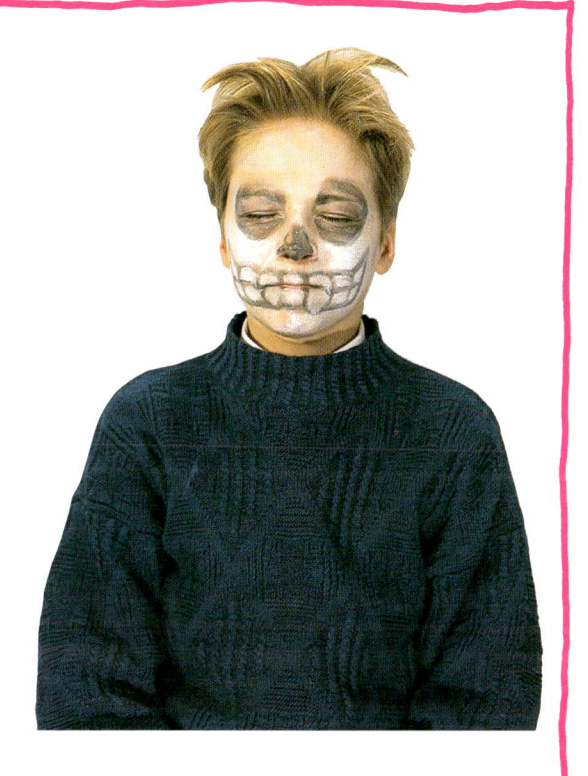

Pirate
The pirate props become much more alarming when they are worn with skeleton make-up.

Tracing

1 Place tracing paper over the outline you want to copy. Secure it with tape if necessary. Draw around the outline.
2 Turn over the tracing paper and rub pencil thickly over the back of the outline.
3 Turn over the tracing paper. Place it over card and re-trace the outline.
4 The outline will be transferred to the card.

Index

bright-eyed robot 14-15

clown 25
Cyclops 11

eagle 16-17
elephant 23

frog 19

glamour specs 7
glitter mask
goggles 6

harlequin mask 5

King Tut 25

Madame Butterfly 6
mouse 22

pirate 25

robot 12-13
rooster 18

skeleton 28-29
sunflower 10

tracing 32